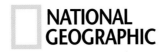

NATIONAL
GEOGRAPHIC

D0503561

What Lives in a Swamp?

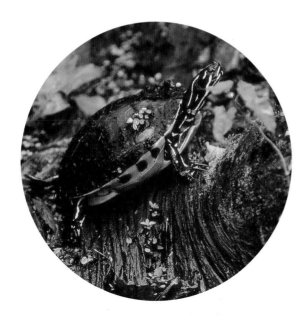

Jacob Fink

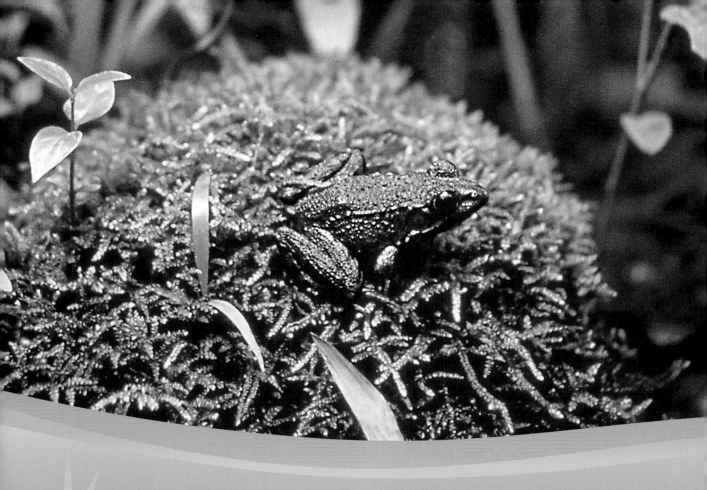

Frogs live in a swamp.

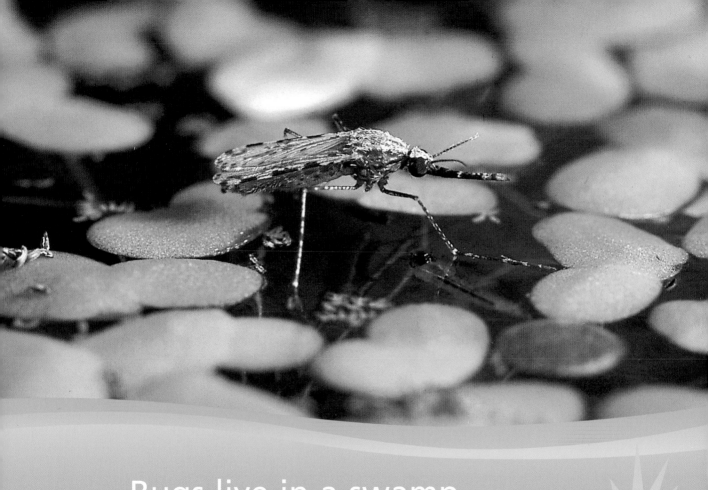

Bugs live in a swamp.

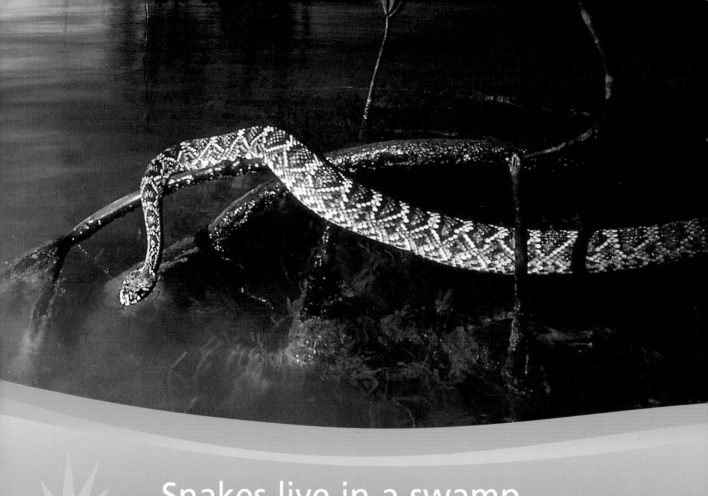

Snakes live in a swamp.

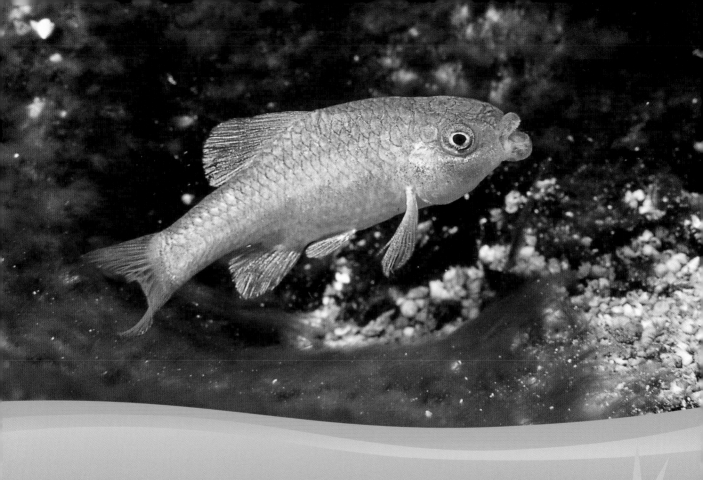

Fish live in a swamp.

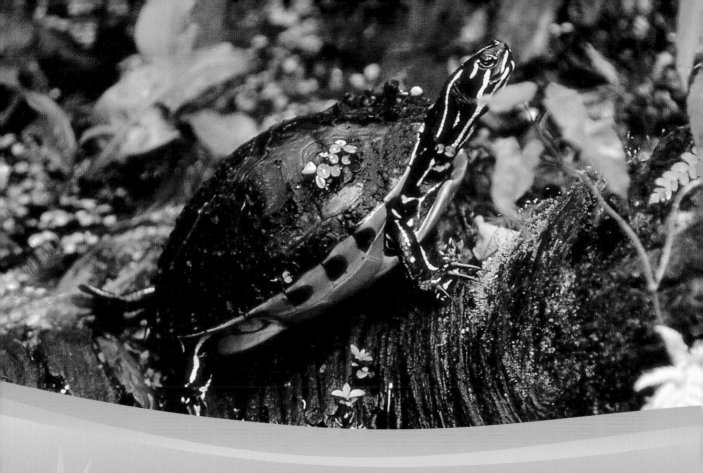

Turtles live in a swamp.

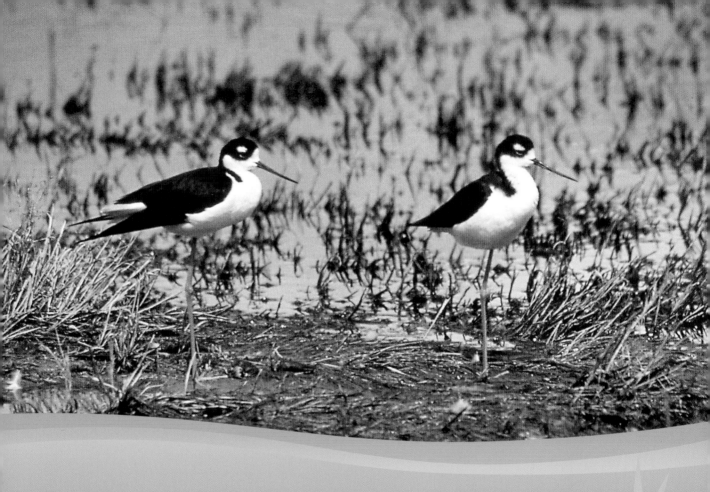

Birds live in a swamp.

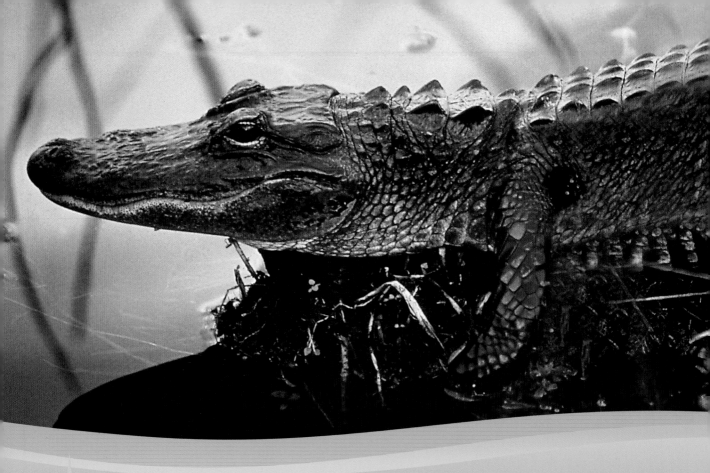

What else lives in a swamp?